W9-BHZ-469

HARRIS COUNTY PUBLIC LIBRARY

J 372.623 Min
Minden, Cecilia
How to write about your
adventure

$24.22
ocn695860260
01/18/2012

WITHDRAWN

How to Write About Your Adventure

by Cecilia Minden
and Kate Roth

CHERRY LAKE PUBLISHING · ANN ARBOR, MICHIGAN

Published in the United States of America by Cherry Lake Publishing
Ann Arbor, Michigan
www.cherrylakepublishing.com

Content Adviser: Jeannette Mancilla-Martinez, EdD, Assistant Professor
of Literacy, Language, and Culture, University of Illinois at Chicago

Design and Illustration: The Design Lab

Photo Credits: Page 5, ©jordache/Shutterstock.com; page 6, ©AVAVA/
Shutterstock.com; page 11, ©Kzenon/Shutterstock.com; page 15,
©Istockphoto.com/DIGIcal; page 20, ©Monkey Business Images/
Shutterstock.com

Copyright ©2012 by Cherry Lake Publishing
All rights reserved. No part of this book may be reproduced or utilized in
any form or by any means without written permission from the publisher.

Library of Congress Cataloging-in-Publication Data
Minden, Cecilia.
  How to write about your adventure/by Cecilia Minden and Kate Roth.
    p. cm.—(Language arts explorer junior)
  Includes bibliographical references and index.
  ISBN-13: 978-1-61080-106-5 (lib. bdg.)
  ISBN-13: 978-1-61080-277-2 (pbk.)
  1. Language arts (Elementary) 2. Narration (Rhetoric)—Juvenile
literature. 3. English language—Composition and exercises—Study and
teaching. I. Roth, Kate. II. Title.
  LB1576.M533 2011
   372.62'3—dc22   2011000164

Cherry Lake Publishing would like to acknowledge the work
of The Partnership for 21st Century Skills. Please visit
www.21stcenturyskills.org for more information.

Printed in the United States of America
Corporate Graphics Inc.
July 2011
CLFA09

Table of Contents

CHAPTER ONE

Sharing Your Story

What great adventures have you had?

Think of the most exciting **adventure** you have ever experienced. Do you want to share your story with other people? Try writing a **personal narrative**!

A personal narrative is a story about something meaningful or special that has happened to the author. The author is represented by the pronoun *I*. This is called writing in the first person.

Personal narratives let you share your experiences with other people.

CHAPTER TWO

Write About What You Know!

Looking at photographs can help you remember exciting events in your life.

Your personal narrative should focus on a single experience or adventure. Look at photographs. Talk to your family and friends. Narrow down possible **topics** for your personal narrative. Choose one to bring to life for other people!

You can't include every single detail of your adventure. If you did, your personal narrative would become a list! Instead, focus on the part that is the most interesting or exciting. It is helpful to list any **events** that occurred in **chronological** order. Think of a hill. You want your personal narrative to build up to the most exciting part of your adventure. What details can you add to build up your story?

Plan Your Adventure Story!

HERE'S WHAT YOU'LL NEED:
- Any photographs of your adventure
- A pencil and paper (or a computer and a printer)

INSTRUCTIONS:
1. Talk to your family and friends about events you have shared, and look at photographs of adventures you have experienced.
2. List three experiences that you would enjoy sharing with others.
3. Pick one topic to write about.
4. Focus on the most interesting part of this adventure.
5. Now write a list of all the events that made your adventure exciting.
6. Put the list in chronological order.

Sample Topic List

Topic Ideas:

1. Marching in a parade
2. Riding a horse
3. Whale watching

Sample List of Chronological Events

Whale-Watching Events:

1. I went whale watching with my family.
2. There were no whales at first.
3. Then whales came by our boat.
4. We saw whales jumping.
5. My brother took a great photo of a jumping whale.
6. My brother almost fell into the water.

CHAPTER THREE

How Did It Begin?

Whale watching is one kind of adventure.

Close your eyes and think about how your adventure began. Your opening should make readers feel the same way you did at that moment. They should want to learn more about your experience after reading your opening.

What did you see, smell, hear, and feel when your adventure started? Were you excited or scared? Write a few sentences about what you experienced. Choose the one that would be the best opening!

Think about the first part of your adventure. What do you remember?

ACTIVITY

Write Your Opening!

HERE'S WHAT YOU'LL NEED:
- Any photographs of your adventure
- A pencil and paper (or a computer and a printer)

INSTRUCTIONS:
1. Think about how your adventure began. Looking at your photographs again may be helpful.
2. Write three possible openings for your story.
3. Pick the one that will make readers most interested in reading about your adventure.

Sample Openings

Opening Ideas:

1. The morning sky was just starting to get light. It was cold and rainy. We waited in line with the other passengers. Finally, we were allowed on the boat. Now we could see the whales!

2. The drizzling rain froze our hands and noses while we waited on the dock. At last, the call came: All Aboard! My family and I were off on our whale-watching adventure.

3. I was so excited to go whale watching! My family and I stood with other passengers in the rain until we could get on the boat. Soon it was time to climb aboard and search for some whales!

CHAPTER FOUR

What Happened Next?

Try to remember as many details as you can.

Now start writing the **body** of your personal narrative. Imagine your story as a movie in your mind. What important details do you include? Keep adding details to your narrative that will help readers experience what you did. Use words like *after* and *then* to show the chronology of events. Including dialogue also helps bring your story to life!

Be sure to explain the main problem or situation in your adventure. As you tell your story, build toward the **climax**. The climax is the turning point just before the main problem is solved or an important event occurs.

The climax of a story is a lot like the very top of a roller coaster before a big drop.

Write the Body!

HERE'S WHAT YOU'LL NEED:
- Any photographs of your adventure
- Your list of chronological events
- A pencil and paper (or a computer and a printer)

INSTRUCTIONS:
1. Look at your photographs and list of chronological events.
2. Continue adding details to your story that build toward the climax.
3. Keep these tips in mind:
   - Keep your story focused.
   - Use words to show the passage of time.
   - Use the first person.
   - Include dialogue to help bring your adventure to life.

Sample Body

    I thought we would see whales right away. We didn't for about an hour. Then the captain came on the loudspeaker. "Whales in sight!" he called.

    We all rushed up on deck to see the whales. I thought the boat might tip with everyone leaning over one side! My big brother, Sam, and I moved to the front of the crowd. He stretched over the railing to get a picture of the whales.

    Just as a whale jumped above the waves, my mom screamed, "Sam, get back!" Sam lost his balance and dropped the camera. Luckily, my dad grabbed Sam. I grabbed the camera.

CHAPTER FIVE

How Did It End?

The ending of a personal narrative includes a **resolution**. This part of the story tells how the main problem was solved or what happened after the main event occurred. It lets readers know how your adventure ended.

After you finish writing your resolution, give your personal narrative a title. Try to keep it short. Choose words that will catch readers' attention.

ACTIVITY

Write the Ending and the Title!

HERE'S WHAT YOU'LL NEED:
- Your list of chronological events
- A pencil and paper (or a computer and a printer)

INSTRUCTIONS:
1. Write the resolution to your story.
2. Read your story aloud to listen to how it sounds.
3. Write three possible titles.
4. Choose the title that you think will do the best job of getting the reader's attention.

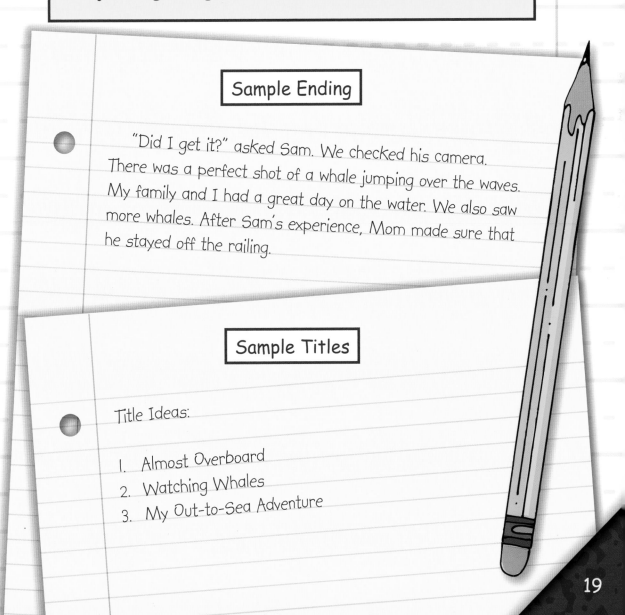

Sample Ending

"Did I get it?" asked Sam. We checked his camera. There was a perfect shot of a whale jumping over the waves. My family and I had a great day on the water. We also saw more whales. After Sam's experience, Mom made sure that he stayed off the railing.

Sample Titles

Title Ideas:

1. Almost Overboard
2. Watching Whales
3. My Out-to-Sea Adventure

CHAPTER SIX

A Final Step Before You Share

Don't forget to reread your personal narrative before you share it with others. Check for any spelling and grammar mistakes. Do you remember other special moments that could become personal narratives?

Reread your work to make sure it is exactly how you want it.

STOP! DON'T WRITE IN THE BOOK!

ACTIVITY

Remember to Review!

Ask yourself these questions as you reread your personal narrative:

☐ YES ☐ NO Do I have an attention-getting title and opening?

☐ YES ☐ NO Do I show readers what I felt and experienced?

☐ YES ☐ NO Do I include dialogue?

☐ YES ☐ NO Do I use words that explain the chronology of events?

☐ YES ☐ NO Do I add details that help build the story to the climax?

☐ YES ☐ NO Do I include a resolution in my ending?

☐ YES ☐ NO Do I use correct grammar and spelling?

Glossary

adventure (ad-VEN-chur) a wild or exciting activity or event

body (BAH-dee) the main part of a personal narrative

chronological (kra-nuh-LA-ji-kuhl) following the order in which events occur

climax (KLI-maks) the turning point in a story that occurs just before the resolution

dialogue (DI-uh-log) spoken words between two or more people

events (ee-VENTS) things that occur at set places and times

personal narrative (PUR-suh-nuhl NER-uh-tiv) a first-person story about something meaningful that has happened to the author

resolution (reh-zuh-LU-shuhn) the part of a personal narrative that tells how the story ends

topics (TAH-piks) subjects

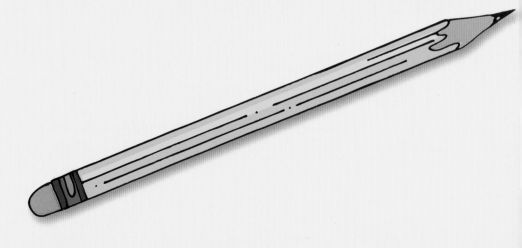

For More Information

BOOKS

Fletcher, Ralph J. *How to Write Your Life Story*. New York: Collins, 2007.

Jarnow, Jill. *Writing to Retell*. New York: PowerKids Press, 2006.

WEB SITE

TIME for Kids—Personal Narrative
www.timeforkids.com/TFK/kids/hh/writeideas/ articles/0,28372,606653,00.html
Check out this site for additional tips on writing a personal narrative.

Index

About the Authors

Cecilia Minden, PhD, is the former director of the Language and Literacy Program at Harvard Graduate School of Education. She earned her doctorate from the University of Virginia. While at Harvard, Dr. Minden also taught several writing courses. Her research focuses on early literacy skills and developing phonics curriculums. She is now a full-time literacy consultant and the author of more than 100 books for children. Dr. Minden lives with her family in Chapel Hill, North Carolina. She likes to write early in the morning while the house is still quiet.

Kate Roth has a doctorate from Harvard University in language and literacy and a master's degree from Columbia University Teachers College in curriculum and teaching. Her work focuses on writing instruction in the primary grades. She has taught kindergarten, first grade, and Reading Recovery. She has also instructed hundreds of teachers around the world in early-literacy practices. She lives in Shanghai, China, with her husband and three children, ages 2, 6, and 9. Together they do a lot of writing to stay in touch with friends and family and to record their experiences.

HARRIS COUNTY PUBLIC LIBRARY
HOUSTON, TEXAS